Step by Step

T0011684

The Story of Syrup

It Starts with a Maple Tree

Melanie Mitchell

Lerner Publications ◆ Minneapolis

Lerner Publications Company
An imprint of Lerner Publishing Group, Inc.
241 First Avenue North
Minneapolis, MN 55401 USA

For reading levels and more information, look up this title at www.lernerbooks.com.

Image credits: JGI/Jamie Grill/Getty Images, p. 3; Dmitrii Bykanov/Getty Images, pp. 5, 23 (lower right); Erin Paul Donovan, p. 7; sianc/Shutterstock.com, p. 9; Stan Tekiela Author/Naturalist/Wildlife Photographer/Getty Images, pp. 11, 23 (lower left); Mr. Tobin/Shutterstock.com, p. 13; ImageInnovation/Getty Images, p. 15; Andre Jenny/Alamy Stock Photo, pp. 17, 23 (top left); DGPICTURE/Shutterstock.com, pp. 19, 23 (top right); Andrew Cline/Shutterstock.com, p. 21; Moyo Studio/Getty Images, p. 22. Cover images: vvoe/Shutterstock.com (branch); Yuriy Golub/Shutterstock.com (pancakes).

Main body text set in Mikado a Medium. Typeface provided by HVD Fonts.

Library of Congress Cataloging-in-Publication Data

Names: Mitchell, Melanie (Melanie S.) author.
Title: The story of syrup : it starts with a maple tree / Melanie Mitchell.
Other titles: From maple tree to syrup
Description: Minneapolis : Lerner Publications, 2022 | Series: Step by step | Includes bibliographical references and index. | Audience: Ages 4–8 | Audience: Grades K–1 | Summary: "From the trunk of a maple tree to the syrup on a stack of pancakes, discover how this sweet treat is made. Detailed photos and clear text illustrate each step in the process"— Provided by publisher.
Identifiers: LCCN 2020058543 (print) | LCCN 2020058544 (ebook) | ISBN 9781728428215 (library binding) | ISBN 9781728431680 (paperback) | ISBN 9781728430850 (ebook)
Subjects: LCSH: Maple syrup—Juvenile literature.
Classification: LCC TP395 .M57 2022 (print) | LCC TP395 (ebook) | DDC 664/.132—dc23

LC record available at https://lccn.loc.gov/2020058543
LC ebook record available at https://lccn.loc.gov/2020058544

Manufactured in the United States of America
1-49358-49462-3/18/2021

Maple syrup is sweet. How is it made?

Workers plant maple trees.

The trees grow.

Workers drill holes.

Spouts are put in
the holes.

Workers hang buckets.

The buckets are emptied.

The barrels are taken away.

The sap is heated.

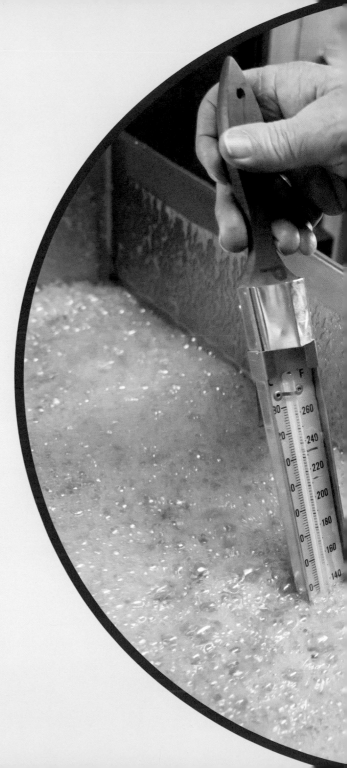

The maple syrup
is poured.

Time to eat!

Picture Glossary

barrel

sap

spout

worker

Learn More

Hansen, Grace. *How Is Maple Syrup Made?* Minneapolis: Abdo Kids, 2019.

Knowlton, Laurie Lazzaro. *Maple Syrup from the Sugarhouse.* Chicago: Albert Whitman, 2017.

Peters, Katie. *Let's Look at Apple Trees.* Minneapolis: Lerner Publications, 2021.

Index